steam it!

steam it!

for meals that taste the way nature intended

Love Food ® is an imprint of Parragon Books Ltd

Parragon
Queen Street House
4 Queen Street
Bath BA1 1HE, UK

ISBN: 978-1-4075-3400-8

Printed in China

Recipes and introduction written by Linda Doeser
Designed by Andrew Easton at Ummagumma
Photography by Charlie Richards
Food styling by Lucy Jessop

Notes for the Reader

This book uses imperial, metric, and U.S. cup measurements. Follow the same units of measurement throughout; do not mix imperial and metric. All spoon measurements are level: teaspoons are assumed to be 5 ml, and tablespoons are assumed to be 15 ml. Unless otherwise stated, milk is assumed to be whole, eggs and individual vegetables, such as potatoes, are medium, and pepper is freshly ground black pepper.

The times given are an approximate guide only. Preparation times differ according to the techniques used by different people and the cooking times may also vary from those given as a result of the type of oven used. Optional ingredients, variations, or serving suggestions have not been included in the calculations.

Recipes using raw or very lightly cooked eggs should be avoided by infants, the elderly, pregnant women, convalescents, and anyone with a chronic condition. Pregnant and breastfeeding women are advised to avoid eating peanuts and peanut products. People with nut allergies should be aware that some of the prepared ingredients used in the recipes in this book may contain nuts. Always check the packaging before use.

contents

introduction

Many more kinds of foods can be cooked by the gentle method of steaming than most people realize—from vegetable medleys to layered terrines, from whole fish to hearty casseroles, and from fluffy grains to creamy desserts. Forget any preconceptions about heavy pot pies and discover that winter warmers, whether sweet or savory, can be light and airy as well as full of flavor.

Steaming is the perfect technique for today's health-conscious and busy cooks. It retains far more nutrients than other methods of cooking and does not require added fat or oil. The color and texture of ingredients are retained, and it is an ideal way of cooking delicate foods, such as fish. Although not invariably the case, many types of food, such as fresh

seafood, and thin cuts of meat, are cooked extremely quickly, and because you can stack steamers over each other, steaming can also be very economical with fuel.

Steaming methods

A traditional method of steaming is to put the ingredients directly into a steamer basket—a perforated metal container—cover it with a tight-fitting lid, and set it over a saucepan of boiling water. This simple technique is still a useful one for a lot of foods. However, for extra flavor, other liquids, such as stock or reserved marinade, can be substituted for water and these can then sometimes be used as the basis for a sauce to serve with the dish. Adding aromatic herbs, spices, or citrus rind to plain water also enhances the flavor of the food.

A second classic method of steaming is to put the food in a container, such as a ovenproof bowl or ramekin, cover it with wax paper and/or aluminum foil, and

put it in the steamer. Traditional sweet and savory pies and sponge cake-based desserts are cooked this way and it also works well for stews, mixed vegetable dishes, fruits, and egg custards.

A variation of this method is to stand the covered bowl on an upturned plate or a trivet inside a large saucepan of boiling water. This prevents it from being in direct contact with the heat source. Make sure that the water comes no more than halfway up the side of the container and that there is plenty of room for the steam to circulate. Remember to cover the pan.

Ingredients that require a longer cooking time, such as thick cuts of meat and whole fish, need extra protection, because otherwise they may dry out in spite of the moist atmosphere in the steamer. Wrapping the food in a wax paper or foil parcel keeps it moist and seals in the nutrients and flavor. You can also use a variety of leaves, such as Swiss chard, lettuce, or banana, or corn husks for wrapping, some of which are edible and all of which look appealing.

Rice and other grains are usually steamed in a slightly different way. The rice and a measured

Types of steamers

Almost all steamers require three components: a container for the boiling liquid—usually a saucepan or wok—a steaming compartment, and a tight-fitting lid.

• Tiered steamers are usually made of aluminum, have a perforated bottom, and are designed with a series of graduated ridges along the sides to fit a wide variety of saucepan sizes. They may be stacked so that different ingredients can be steamed simultaneously. They are often supplied with a domed lid. Electrical models are available with a thermostatically controlled heating element under the bottom container for the liquid.

• Flexible steamer baskets are usually made of steel with adjustable folding sides and short legs that stand on the bottom of a saucepan. They come in a range of sizes to fit most saucepans and are very adaptable. Make sure that the saucepan has a tight-fitting lid.

• Bamboo steamers are designed to rest against the side of a wok

quantity of cold water are put into a saucepan so that the rice is covered by about 1 inch /2.5 cm. When the water comes to a boil, the heat is reduced to a simmer, the pan is covered with a tight-fitting lid, and the rice is left to steam for 15–20 minutes, until all the

liquid has been absorbed. The pan is then removed from the heat and left to stand for a few minutes, still covered, for the rice to finish steaming. Live shellfish, such as mussels and clams, are steamed in a similar way, although with less liquid and for a shorter time.

about 2 inches/5 cm above the water level. These attractive Chinese baskets can be stacked in a tower and are supplied with a tight-fitting bamboo lid. They are available from Asian supermarkets and stores.

Dos and don'ts

- Do not let the boiling liquid touch the steaming compartment.
- Do not let the pan boil dry. Check every 15–20 minutes and add boiling water or stock, as required.
- Do ensure you always cover the steamer with a tight-fitting lid.
- Do keep an eye on the cooking time, because the heat during steaming is intense and it is easy to overcook food. Become familiar with your own steamer— timings given in the recipes are only guidelines to follow.
- Do not leave food in the steamer after cooking, even with the heat turned off, because it will continue to cook and this will possibly ruin the dish.

fish &
shellfish

rolled fillets of sole

SERVES 4

4 sole, filleted and skinned
2 tbsp olive oil
1 tbsp white wine vinegar
2 tbsp finely chopped fresh
  parsley

1 zucchini, grated
1 carrot, grated
1 onion, very finely chopped
4 tbsp fresh white breadcrumbs
1 tbsp lemon juice

scant 2 cups fish stock
2/3 cup white wine
salt and pepper
fresh parsley sprigs, to garnish

Put the sole fillets into a shallow, nonmetallic dish. Combine the oil, vinegar, and parsley and pour the mixture over the fish. Cover with plastic wrap and let marinate for 30 minutes.

Combine the zucchini, carrot, onion, breadcrumbs, and lemon juice in a bowl and season to taste with salt and pepper.

Pour the fish stock and white wine into a pan and bring to a boil. Meanwhile, drain the fish, pat dry with paper towels, and season with salt and

pepper. Divide the vegetable stuffing evenly among the fish fillets and roll up. Place the fish rolls in a single layer in a heatproof dish that will fit inside the steamer.

Place the steamer over the pan of boiling stock and cover with a tight-fitting lid. Steam for about 8 minutes, until the flesh flakes easily. Remove from the steamer and serve immediately, garnished with parsley sprigs.

chinese steamed sea bream

SERVES 4

1 sea bream, about 2 lb 4 oz/1 kg,
   scaled and cleaned
1 tsp salt
2 garlic cloves, finely chopped
1 bunch scallions, shredded
2 tbsp grated fresh ginger

pinch of superfine sugar
$1\frac{1}{2}$ tbsp sesame oil
$1\frac{1}{2}$ tbsp peanut oil
shredded scallions and lemon
   slices, to garnish
light soy sauce, to serve

Bring a pan of water to a boil. Meanwhile, rinse the fish well under cold running water and pat dry with paper towels. Slash the flesh diagonally several times on both sides and rub in the salt. Put the fish in a heatproof dish or on a deep plate that will fit inside the steamer.

Tuck the garlic, one-third of the scallions, and half the ginger inside the cavity of the fish. Place the dish in the steamer and cover with a tight-fitting lid.

Set the steamer over the pan of boiling water and steam for about 20 minutes, until the flesh flakes easily.

Remove the dish from the steamer and sprinkle the fish with the sugar, remaining scallions, and remaining ginger.

Heat the oils in a small pan and when hot, gently pour the mixture over the fish. Serve immediately, garnished with shredded scallions and lemon slices and accompanied by a small dish of light soy sauce.

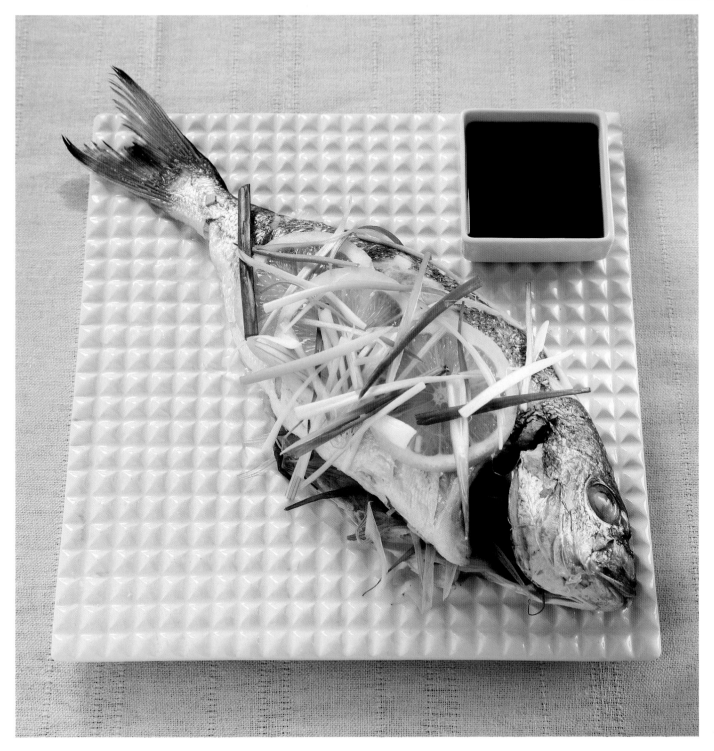

monkfish in swiss chard parcels

SERVES 4

1 lb 2 oz/500 g Swiss chard,
   trimmed
1 lb 4 oz/550 g monkfish fillet,
   cut into bite-size pieces
1 1/2 tbsp lime juice
2/3 cup crème fraîche or sour cream

2 egg yolks, lightly beaten
pinch of paprika
3 tbsp butter
1/2 cup white wine
salt and pepper

Cut off the chard leaves, reserving the stems. Steam 8 leaves for 15 seconds, then remove and spread out on a counter. Shred any remaining leaves.

Combine the pieces of fish, lime juice, and 5 tablespoons of the crème fraîche in a bowl. Stir in the egg yolks, add the paprika, and season to taste.

Divide the fish mixture equally among the steamed leaves, then roll up, tucking in the sides. Secure with toothpicks or tie with kitchen string.

Bring a pan of water to a boil and line a steamer with wax paper. Put the rolls in the steamer in a single layer, cover with a tight-fitting lid, and steam for 15–20 minutes, until tender.

Meanwhile, finely chop the reserved stalks. Melt the butter in the skillet, add the chard stalks, and cook over low heat, stirring occasionally, for 10 minutes, until tender. Stir in the white wine and bring to a boil.

Transfer the chard mixture to a blender or food processor, add the remaining crème fraîche, and process until smooth. Scrape the mixture into a pan, add the shredded chard leaves, and cook over low heat, stirring constantly, until thickened. Season to taste with salt and pepper.

Remove the fish parcels from the steamer and transfer to a serving dish. Spoon the sauce into the dish and serve immediately.

marinated salmon with chili sauce

SERVES 4

4 salmon fillets, about
  6 oz/175 g each
4 scallions, chopped
1 lemongrass stalk, chopped
1 tbsp finely chopped fresh ginger
2 fresh red chiles, seeded and
  finely chopped
2 tbsp Thai fish sauce
fresh cilantro sprigs, to garnish
steamed greens and lime wedges,
  to serve

marinade
juice of 1 lime
2 tbsp Chinese rice wine or dry
  sherry
3 tbsp chopped fresh cilantro
2 garlic cloves, finely chopped

chili sauce
12 fresh red chiles, seeded and
  coarsely chopped
3 garlic cloves, finely chopped
1 tbsp brown sugar
juice of 1 lime
4 tbsp Thai fish sauce

Put the salmon fillets in a shallow dish. Combine all the marinade ingredients and pour over the fish. Turn to coat, cover with plastic wrap, and let marinate for 30 minutes.

Meanwhile, make the chili sauce. Put all the ingredients into a food processor or blender and process until thoroughly blended. Scrape the sauce into a small serving bowl and set aside until required.

Bring a pan of water to a boil. Meanwhile, line a steamer with wax paper. Drain the salmon fillets, reserving the marinade, and put them in the steamer in a single layer. Add the scallions, lemongrass, ginger, chiles, and Thai fish sauce to the reserved marinade and mix well. Spoon the mixture evenly over the fish.

Cover the steamer with a tight-fitting lid and set it over the pan. Steam for 10 minutes, until the fish flakes easily.

Lift the fish fillets out of the steamer and put them onto warmed serving plates. Garnish with the cilantro sprigs and serve immediately with the chili sauce, steamed greens and lime wedges.

seafood & lemongrass skewers

SERVES 4

8 lemongrass stalks
1 tbsp peanut oil
2 tbsp lemon juice
1 tbsp finely chopped fresh mint
1 tsp green peppercorns

24 raw jumbo shrimp, peeled and
 deveined
12 large scallops, shucked and
 halved
1$\frac{1}{4}$ cups water

salt and pepper
chopped fresh mint, to garnish
lemon wedges, to serve

Remove the outer leaves from the lemongrass stalks. Cut off and finely chop the bulbous base of the stalks and put into a bowl. Reserve the stalks. Add the oil, lemon juice, chopped mint, and peppercorns to the bowl, mix well, and season with salt and pepper.

Thread the shrimp and scallops alternately onto the lemongrass stalks and place in a large, shallow nonmetallic dish. Pour the marinade over them and turn to coat. Cover with plastic wrap and set aside in a cool place for 30 minutes.

Line a steamer with wax paper. Drain the skewers, reserving the marinade, and put into the steamer. Cover with a tight-fitting lid. Pour the marinade into a pan, add 1$\frac{1}{4}$ cups water, and bring to a boil. Set the steamer over the pan and steam for 10 minutes, until the seafood is cooked through and tender.

Remove the skewers from the steamer and serve immediately, garnished with chopped mint and lemon wedges.

shellfish medley with radicchio cream

SERVES 4

1¼ cups fish stock
1 lb/450 g live mussels
8 oz/225 g live clams
12 raw jumbo shrimp
4 oz/115 g sugar snap peas, trimmed

12 baby carrots, trimmed
½ daikon, cut into ½-inch/1-cm slices
8 scallops, shucked and halved
4 tbsp lemon juice
2 tbsp chopped fresh parsley

1 head radicchio, coarsely chopped
3 tbsp crème fraîche or sour cream
salt and pepper
chopped fresh parsley, to garnish
lemon wedges, to serve

Pour the stock into a pan and bring to a boil. Meanwhile, scrub the mussels and clams under cold running water and pull off the "beards" from the mussels. Discard any shellfish with broken or damaged shells and any that do not shut immediately when sharply tapped.

Put the shrimp into a steamer, cover with a tight-fitting lid, and set over the pan of boiling stock. Steam for 5 minutes, then remove from the heat, and let cool slightly. When cool enough to handle, peel the shrimp and add the shells and heads to the fish stock. Bring the stock back to a boil, then reduce the heat and simmer for 10 minutes. Devein the shrimp, then halve them and set aside.

Remove the shrimp heads and shells from the stock with a slotted spoon and discard. Put the sugar snap peas, carrots, and daikon into the steamer, cover with a tight-fitting lid, set over the boiling stock, and steam for 5 minutes.

Add the mussels, clams, shrimp, and scallops to the steamer and sprinkle with the lemon juice and parsley. Re-cover and steam for 5 minutes more. Transfer the shellfish medley to a dish and keep warm. Discard any mussels or clams that remain closed.

Add the radicchio to the stock, increase the heat to high, and boil rapidly until the liquid has reduced by half. Remove the pan from the heat and let cool slightly, then transfer the mixture to a blender or food processor. Add the crème fraîche and process until smooth. Season to taste with salt and pepper.

Pour the sauce into a warm serving dish. Top with the shellfish medley, garnish with chopped parsley and serve immediately with lemon wedges.

shrimp wraps with spicy salsa

SERVES 4–6

1 lb/450 g cooked peeled shrimp
4 tbsp lime juice
2 tbsp chopped fresh cilantro
1 fresh red chile, seeded and
  finely chopped
2/3 cup sour cream
1 bunch scallions, finely chopped

4 mixed red and yellow bell
  peppers, seeded and finely
  chopped
4 zucchini, diced
8 oz/225 g baby corn, thickly
  sliced
8–12 flour tortillas
salt and pepper

spicy salsa
2 avocados
4 scallions, finely chopped
2 fresh red chiles, seeded and
  finely chopped
2 tbsp olive oil
4 tbsp lime juice
2 tbsp chopped fresh cilantro

Put the shrimp into a nonmetallic bowl. Combine the lime juice, half the chopped cilantro, and the chile in a pitcher. Pour the mixture over the shrimp, stir gently to coat, cover with plastic wrap, and let marinate in a cool place for 30 minutes.

Combine the sour cream and scallions in a small bowl, cover, and set aside in the refrigerator until ready to serve.

Bring a pan of water to a boil. Put the red and yellow bell peppers, zucchini, and corn in a steamer, cover with a tight-fitting lid, and set over the pan of boiling water. Steam for 5 minutes.

Drain the shrimp, add to the vegetables, re-cover the steamer, and steam for 3–5 minutes more, until heated through.

Heat the tortillas. Stack and warm in a preheated oven at 375°F/190°C for 5 minutes, or heat individually in a skillet, turning once, until lightly browned on both sides. Wrap in foil and keep warm.

Transfer the shrimp and vegetable mixture to a warm serving dish, season to taste with salt and pepper, and keep warm while you make the salsa.

Halve and pit the avocados. Scoop out the flesh, dice finely, and put into a bowl. Add the scallions and chiles. Whisk together the olive oil, lime juice, and cilantro in a pitcher and pour the dressing over the mixture. Toss gently to mix.

Serve everything immediately. Each diner can spread a little scallion cream on a tortilla, top with the shrimp and vegetable mixture, add a spoonful of spicy salsa, and roll up to eat.

mussels steamed in vermouth

SERVES 4

2 tbsp olive oil
6 large shallots, finely chopped
2 garlic cloves, finely chopped
2 fennel bulbs, finely chopped,
4 lb 8 oz/2 kg live mussels

1¼ cups dry vermouth, such as
    Noilly Prat
pepper
French bread, to serve

Heat the oil in a large pan. Add the shallots, garlic, and fennel, cover, and cook over low heat, stirring occasionally, for 8–10 minutes, until softened.

Meanwhile, scrub the mussels under cold running water and pull off the "beards." Discard any shellfish with broken or damaged shells and any that do not shut immediately when sharply tapped. Finely chop the fennel fronds.

Pour the vermouth into the pan and season with pepper. Bring to a boil, add the mussels, cover, and cook over medium–high heat, gently shaking the pan occasionally, for about 5 minutes, until the mussels have opened. Discard any that remain closed.

Divide the mussels and their cooking liquid among individual soup bowls, sprinkle with the chopped fennel fronds, and serve immediately with French bread.

meat &
poultry

meatballs with tomato & thyme sauce

SERVES 4

1 tbsp olive oil
1/2 red onion, finely chopped
2 garlic cloves, finely chopped
1 lb/450 g lean ground steak
1/2 cup fresh white breadcrumbs
1 egg, lightly beaten
cornstarch, for dusting

salt and pepper
fresh sprig of thyme, to garnish
freshly cooked pasta, to serve
  (optional)

tomato sauce
14 oz/400 g canned chopped
  tomatoes
2/3 cup beef stock
2 tsp chopped fresh thyme
1 garlic clove, finely chopped
pinch of sugar

Heat the oil in a skillet. Add the onion and garlic and cook over low heat, stirring occasionally, for 5 minutes, until softened. Remove the skillet from the heat and transfer the onion and garlic to a bowl.

Add the ground steak, breadcrumbs, and egg, season with salt and pepper, and mix well until thoroughly combined. Dust your hands with cornstarch and shape the mixture into 1 1/2-inch/4-cm balls.

Put all the sauce ingredients into a pan, season with salt and pepper, and bring to a boil, stirring occasionally. Reduce the heat to a simmer. Put the meatballs into a steamer, cover with a tight-fitting lid, and set the steamer over the pan. Steam for 10–15 minutes, until the meatballs are cooked through.

Transfer the meatballs to a serving a dish and keep warm. Ladle the sauce into a blender or food processor and process until smooth. Pour the sauce over the meatballs and garnish with the thyme sprig. Serve immediately with pasta, if you like.

pork dim sum

SERVES 4

2 dried Chinese mushrooms
3 oz/85 g lean ground pork
2 tbsp drained canned chopped
    bamboo shoots
1 tsp light brown sugar
1 tsp sesame oil

$^1/_2$ tsp Chinese rice wine or dry
    sherry
$1^1/_2$ tsp soy sauce, plus extra to
    serve
1 tsp cornstarch
scallion slices, to garnish

dumpling dough
$1^1/_4$ cups self-rising flour, plus
    extra for dusting
$^1/_4$ cup boiling water
$1^1/_2$ tsp peanut oil

Put the dried mushrooms in a heatproof bowl, add hot water to cover, and let soak for 20 minutes.

Meanwhile, make the dough. Sift the flour into a bowl and stir in the boiling water. Add the peanut oil and $1-1^1/_2$ tbsp cold water and mix to a dough. Turn out onto a lightly floured counter and knead until smooth. Divide the dough into 16 equal pieces and press out into circles or squares.

Drain the mushrooms and finely chop. Combine the mushrooms, ground pork, bamboo shoots, sugar, sesame oil, rice wine, soy sauce, and cornstarch in a bowl.

Divide the filling among the dough wrappers, placing it in the center of each. Pinch the edges of the dough together to make little pouches.

Bring a pan of water to a boil and line a steamer with damp wax paper.

Put the pouches in a single layer in the steamer and cover with a tight-fitting lid. Set the steamer over the pan and steam for 10–15 minutes. Serve immediately, garnished with scallion slices and with a small dish of soy sauce for dipping.

lamb & bean stew

SERVES 4

1¼ cups black-eyed peas, soaked
   overnight in cold water and
   drained
3 tbsp sunflower oil
2 lb 4 oz/1 kg boneless leg of
   lamb, cut into cubes

4 leeks, sliced
1 parsnip, cut into cubes
3 carrots, thickly sliced
2 small turnips, cut into cubes
⅔ cup veal or beef stock
2 tbsp chopped fresh parsley

1 small fresh rosemary sprig
1 tbsp mint jelly
salt and pepper

Put the peas into a pan, add cold water to cover, and bring to a boil. Boil vigorously for 15 minutes, then drain and set aside.

Meanwhile, heat the oil in a large skillet. Add the meat and cook over medium heat, stirring frequently, for about 8 minutes, until browned all over. Remove with a slotted spoon and set aside.

Add the leeks, parsnip, carrots, and turnips to the skillet and cook, stirring frequently, for about 8 minutes, until softened and beginning to color. Remove with a slotted spoon and set aside.

Pour the stock into the skillet, add the parsley, rosemary, and mint jelly, and bring to a boil, scraping up the sediment from the bottom. Remove the skillet from the heat.

Bring a pan of water to a boil. Combine the lamb, vegetables, and peas, season with salt and pepper, and spoon into a 5-cup heatproof bowl. Pour in the stock mixture. Cut a circle of foil 2 inches/5 cm larger than the circumference of the top of the bowl, make a pleat in the center, and put it over the bowl. Tie in place with string.

Put the bowl into a steamer, cover with a tight-fitting lid, and set it over the pan. Steam for 1¾ hours.

Transfer the lamb, vegetables, and peas to a warm serving dish with a slotted spoon. Remove and discard the rosemary sprig. If the remaining stock mixture is too thin, pour it into a pan and boil until reduced and thickened. Taste and adjust the seasoning and pour it over the stew. Serve immediately.

herbed leg of lamb with vegetables

SERVES 6

1 tbsp sunflower oil
1 onion, thinly sliced
2 leeks, thinly sliced
2 carrots, thinly sliced
2 celery stalks, thinly sliced

3 lb 5-oz/1.5-kg leg of lamb, boned
4 garlic cloves, thinly sliced
2 fresh rosemary sprigs, plus extra to garnish

$^2/_3$ cup veal or beef stock
$^1/_4$ cup rosé wine
2 tbsp mint jelly
salt and pepper

Cut a sheet of foil large enough to enclose the lamb completely. Heat the oil in a skillet. Add the onion, leeks, carrots, and celery and cook over low heat, stirring occasionally, for 5 minutes. Using a slotted spoon, transfer the vegetables to the foil to make an even bed.

Meanwhile, make small slits all over the lamb with a small sharp knife. Push a slice of garlic and a few rosemary leaves into each slit.

Add the lamb to the skillet, increase the heat to medium, and cook, turning occasionally, for about 8 minutes, until lightly browned all over. Remove from the skillet and put the lamb on top of the vegetables. Fold up the sides of the foil but do not seal the parcel.

Pour the stock into the skillet and bring to a boil, scraping up the sediment from the bottom. Add

the wine and mint jelly and season with salt and pepper. Spoon the stock mixture over the lamb and seal the edges of the foil. Place the parcel in a steamer and cover with a tight-fitting lid.

Bring a pan of water to a boil. Set the steamer over the pan and steam for $1^1/_2$ hours.

Remove the parcel from the steamer and unwrap. Put the lamb on a plate and let rest for 10–15 minutes. Meanwhile, put the stock and vegetables into a pan and bring to a boil, then boil until reduced and thickened. Taste and adjust the seasoning if necessary. Remove the pan from the heat.

Carve the lamb into medium thick slices and place on a warmed serving dish. Spoon the vegetables and sauce over it, garnish with rosemary, and serve immediately.

spareribs with black beans

SERVES 4

2 tbsp salted black beans
1 tbsp peanut oil, plus extra for brushing
1 tbsp soy sauce
1 tbsp Chinese rice wine or dry sherry
1 tsp light brown sugar

1 tbsp cornstarch
1 lb 2 oz/500 g pork spareribs, chopped into short lengths
2 fresh red chiles, seeded and sliced
1–2 garlic cloves, finely chopped

Put the beans into a bowl, add cold water to cover, and let soak for 10 minutes, then drain well and mash with a fork.

Meanwhile, bring a pan of water to a boil and brush a heatproof dish that will fit in the steamer with oil.

Heat the oil in a skillet or wok, add the beans, and stir-fry for 1 minute. Add the soy sauce, rice wine, and sugar and stir-fry for 30 seconds. Remove the skillet from the heat and let cool.

Mix the cornstarch to a paste with 2 tbsp cold water in a bowl. When the beans are cold, add the pieces of sparerib, cornstarch paste, chiles, and garlic and mix well.

Put the mixture into the prepared dish and place in a steamer. Cover with a tight-fitting lid, set the steamer over the pan of water, and steam for 30 minutes, until tender. Serve immediately.

chicken & leek parcels

SERVES 4

4 skinless, boneless chicken
    breast portions
1 fresh sage sprig
2 tbsp olive oil
2 tbsp walnut oil

4 tbsp lime juice
2 leeks, thinly sliced
4 tbsp chopped mixed fresh
    herbs, such as sage, flat-leaf
    parsley, and thyme

2 garlic cloves, finely chopped
8 black olives, pitted and chopped
8 capers, chopped
salt and pepper

Put the chicken in a shallow nonmetallic dish and add the sage sprig. Combine the olive and walnut oils and lime juice in a bowl and pour the mixture over the chicken. Turn to coat, then cover with plastic wrap and let marinate in the refrigerator for 2–4 hours. Meanwhile, cut out 4 sheets of foil, each large enough to enclose a chicken portion completely.

Bring a pan of water to a boil. Meanwhile, divide the leeks equally among the sheets of foil. Drain the chicken portions, reserving the marinade but discarding the sage sprig, and season them with salt and pepper. Place one on each pile of leeks.

Combine the chopped herbs, garlic, olives, and capers in a small bowl and divide the mixture among the parcels, spooning it on top of the chicken portions. Fold up the sides of the foil without sealing the edges and spoon in the reserved marinade.

Seal the edges of the parcels and place in a steamer. Cover with a tight-fitting lid and steam for 15–20 minutes, until the chicken is cooked through and tender. Transfer the contents of the parcels to warm individual serving plates, and serve immediately.

chicken spirals with bleu cheese sauce

SERVES 4

4 chicken breast portions
4 tsp sun-dried tomato paste
12 fresh basil leaves, plus extra to
   garnish
2 garlic cloves, finely chopped
2 tbsp snipped fresh chives

2 tbsp butter
salt and pepper

bleu cheese sauce
6 oz/175 g Maytag bleu cheese,
   crumbled

$2\frac{1}{2}$ cups crème fraîche
1 tbsp balsamic vinegar
1 tomato, peeled, seeded, and
   finely chopped
$\frac{1}{2}$ red bell pepper, seeded and
   finely chopped

One at a time, put the chicken breast portions between 2 sheets of plastic wrap or wax paper and beat gently with the side of a rolling pin to flatten. Season each with salt and pepper, then spread evenly with the sun-dried tomato paste. Divide the basil leaves among them, then sprinkle with garlic and chives.

Bring a pan of water to a boil. Meanwhile, roll up each chicken portion, one at a time, spread with butter, and wrap in foil to hold securely. Put them into a steamer and cover with a tight-fitting lid. Set the steamer over the pan and steam for 30–40 minutes, until cooked through and tender.

Remove the rolls from the steamer and set aside to cool completely, still wrapped in the foil.

To make the sauce, put the bleu cheese, crème fraîche, and balsamic vinegar into a blender and process until smooth. Alternatively, beat well in a bowl. Stir in the tomato and bell pepper and season to taste with salt and pepper. Cover and chill until required.

When the chicken rolls are completely cold, unwrap and cut into slices. Spoon the sauce onto individual plates and top with the chicken spirals. Garnish with basil leaves and serve immediately.

duck breasts with apple & plum sauce

SERVES 4

2 crisp apples
lemon juice, for brushing
9 oz/250 g plums, pitted and
   halved
1 red onion, finely chopped

6 back peppercorns, lightly
   crushed
6 juniper berries, lightly crushed
2½ cups red wine
1 tbsp slivovitz, applejack, or
   brandy

4 duck breasts
1 tbsp sunflower oil
4 tbsp heavy cream
⅔ cup chicken stock
salt

Peel and core the apples, then brush with lemon juice to prevent discoloration. Put them into a shallow dish with the plums, onion, peppercorns, juniper berries, red wine, and fruit or plain brandy and mix well. Add the duck and turn to coat. Let marinate in the refrigerator, turning the duck occasionally, for 3 hours.

Drain the duck, reserving the marinade, and pat dry with paper towels. Heat the oil in a heavy skillet, add the duck, and cook over medium heat for about 3 minutes on each side, until golden brown. Remove from the skillet.

Put the duck, apples, and plums in a steamer and cover with a tight-fitting lid. Pour the remaining marinade into a pan, stir in the cream and chicken stock, and bring to a boil. Set the steamer over the pan and steam for 12–15 minutes.

Transfer the duck to warmed serving plates. Slice the apples and add them to the plates with the plums. Keep warm. Bring the wine mixture back to a boil and boil until thickened and reduced. Season to taste with salt and strain. Spoon the sauce over the duck and serve immediately.

vegetables

creamy mushrooms with shallot sauce

SERVES 4

2 tbsp sunflower oil, plus extra for
   brushing
1 small onion, finely chopped
1 lb 2 oz/500 g cremini
   mushrooms, chopped
1 cup fresh white breadcrumbs
2 eggs, lightly beaten

2/3 cup sour cream
salt and pepper
fresh parsley sprigs, to garnish

shallot sauce
4 shallots, finely chopped
4 tbsp red wine vinegar

4 tbsp butter
1/4 cup all-purpose flour
1 1/4 cups vegetable stock
1 tsp lemon juice
2 tsp chopped fresh parsley

Heat the oil in a skillet. Add the onion and cook over low heat, stirring occasionally, for 10 minutes, until softened and beginning to color. Add the mushrooms and cook, stirring occasionally, for 5 minutes more, until the juices they give off have evaporated. Remove the skillet from the heat and let cool slightly.

Meanwhile, bring a pan of water to a boil and brush a 2 1/2-cup heatproof bowl with oil. Cut out a circle of wax paper to cover the top of the bowl.

Stir the breadcrumbs, egg, and sour cream into the cooled mushroom mixture and season with salt and pepper. Spoon the mixture into the prepared bowl, cover with the wax paper, and tie in place with kitchen string.

Place the bowl in a steamer and cover with a tight-fitting lid. Set the steamer over the pan and steam for 1 hour.

Start making the sauce about halfway through the cooking time. Put the shallots and vinegar into a pan and bring to a boil. Continue to boil until the vinegar has almost all evaporated. Add half the butter and when it has melted, stir in the flour. Cook, stirring constantly, for 1 minute, then gradually stir in the stock, a little at a time. Bring to a boil, whisking constantly, then reduce the heat and simmer gently for 15 minutes.

Remove the sauce from the heat and season to taste with salt and pepper. Whisk in the remaining butter and the lemon juice. Stir in the parsley and pour the sauce into a sauceboat.

Remove the mushroom mold from the steamer and discard the wax paper. Place a plate on top of the bowl, invert the two, and turn out the mold. Garnish with parsley and serve immediately with the sauce.

summer vegetable parcels

SERVES 4

12 pearl onions
12 baby carrots
12 radishes
1½ cups snow peas
scant 1 cup shelled baby fava
   beans
2 tsp chopped fresh mint

2 tsp chopped fresh parsley
2 tsp finely grated orange rind
4 tbsp dry white wine
4 tbsp butter
salt and pepper
crusty bread, to serve

Peel and trim the vegetables, as necessary. Bring a pan of water to a boil.

Meanwhile, cut out 4 double thickness circles of wax paper about 12 inches/30 cm in diameter. Divide the vegetables equally among them, placing them on one half of each circle. Season with salt and pepper.

Sprinkle with the mint, parsley, orange rind, and wine and dot with the butter. Fold the paper over and twist the edges to seal. Place the parcels in a steamer and cover with a tight-fitting lid.

Set the steamer over the pan and steam for 10 minutes. Transfer the parcels to individual serving plates and serve immediately with crusty bread.

marinated vegetable medley

SERVES 4

1 Bermuda onion, cut into wedges
1 eggplant, cut into chunks
1 orange bell pepper, seeded and
   cut into chunks
2 zucchini, thickly sliced
1 butternut squash, peeled and
   cut into cubes
16 small mushrooms

$^2/_3$ cup tomato juice
juice of 1 lemon
4 tbsp sunflower oil
1 tbsp Worcestershire sauce
1 fresh red chile, seeded and
   finely chopped
2 garlic cloves, finely chopped
1 tsp grated horseradish

$^1/_2$ tsp celery seeds
2 tsp chopped fresh thyme
1 tbsp chopped fresh parsley
$1^1/_4$ cups vegetable stock
salt and pepper
lemon wedges, to serve

Put the onion, eggplant, bell pepper, zucchini, squash, and mushrooms into a large dish. Combine the tomato juice, lemon juice, sunflower oil, Worcestershire sauce, chile, garlic, horseradish, celery seeds, thyme, and parsley in a bowl and season with salt and pepper. Pour the mixture over the vegetables and toss to coat. Cover the dish with plastic wrap and let marinate in the refrigerator for 4 hours.

Drain the vegetables, reserving the marinade. Pour the marinade into a pan, add the stock, and bring to a boil.

Meanwhile, thread the vegetables onto 8 skewers and put them into a steamer. Cover with a tight-fitting lid, set the steamer over the pan, and steam for 8–10 minutes, until the vegetables are tender.

Transfer the skewers to a warm serving dish. Check the consistency of the marinade and if it is too thin, boil for a few minutes longer to reduce. Pour the marinade into a sauceboat and serve immediately with the kebobs and lemon wedges.

harvesters' pie

SERVES 4

1 small onion, finely chopped
1 parsnip, finely chopped
1 small turnip, finely chopped
1²/₃ cups chopped mushrooms
scant 1 cup drained canned
    cannellini beans

1½ cups grated cheddar or
    Gruyère cheese
1 tsp chopped fresh thyme
2 tbsp all-purpose flour
4 tbsp vegetable stock
salt and pepper

dough
1½ cups all-purpose flour, plus
    extra for dusting
1 tsp baking powder
pinch of salt
6 tbsp butter, diced
1 egg, lightly beaten

First make the dough. Sift together the flour, baking powder, and salt into a bowl. Add the butter and rub in with your fingertips until the mixture resembles fine breadcrumbs. Stir in the egg and just enough water to mix to a firm dough.

Turn out onto a lightly floured counter and knead briefly. Cut off and reserve one-quarter of the dough and roll out the remainder. Use the larger piece of dough to line a 3³/₄-cup heatproof bowl, easing it gently into place. Roll out the smaller piece of dough to make a lid and set aside.

Half fill a pan with water and bring to a boil. Cut out a circle of wax paper and a circle of foil 2 inches/5 cm larger than the top of the bowl. Place them together and make a pleat in the center.

Meanwhile, combine the onion, parsnip, turnip, mushrooms, cannellini beans, and grated cheese

in a bowl. Sprinkle with the thyme and flour, season to taste with salt and pepper, and mix well. Spoon the vegetable mixture into the lined bowl, pressing it down gently. Add the vegetable stock and cover with the dough lid. Put the wax paper and foil circles over the bowl and tie securely with kitchen string.

Carefully put the bowl into a pan of boiling water, which should come about halfway up the side. Cover the pan with a tight-fitting lid and steam for 3 hours. Check the level of the water in the pan frequently and add more boiling water as required.

Lift the bowl out of the pan. Remove and discard the string and wax and foil circles. Place a plate on top of the bowl and, holding them together, invert to turn out the pie. Serve immediately.

focaccia with tomatoes & taleggio

SERVES 4

1 onion, cheese, or herb focaccia
1 tbsp pesto
4 tbsp unsalted butter, at room
   temperature
2 large ripe plum tomatoes,
   peeled and thinly sliced

5 oz/140 g Taleggio cheese,
   thinly sliced
3 eggs
1¼ cups light cream
1 tbsp chopped fresh flat-leaf
   parsley

⅔ cup grated Parmesan cheese
salt and pepper

Slice the focaccia. Beat the pesto and butter together in a small bowl, then spread the mixture over one side of each slice of bread.

Make layers of focaccia, tomatoes, and Taleggio in a heatproof dish that will fit inside the steamer. Lightly beat the eggs in a bowl, then beat in the cream, add the parsley, and season with salt and pepper. Pour the mixture evenly over the contents of the dish and let stand for 30 minutes.

Bring a pan of water to a boil. Cover the dish with foil and put it in the steamer. Cover with a tight-fitting lid and set over the pan. Steam for 40 minutes.

Toward the end of the cooking time, preheat the broiler. Lift the dish out of the steamer and remove and discard the foil. Sprinkle the Parmesan over the surface and cook under the broiler for a few minutes, until golden brown and bubbling.

zucchini & carrot terrine

SERVES 6

2 tbsp peanut oil, plus extra for
  brushing
8 oz/225 g onions, finely chopped
2 garlic cloves, finely chopped

6 cups grated zucchini
scant 1 cup diced carrots
1 lb 10 oz/750 g bok choy,
  trimmed

1 tbsp soy sauce
pinch of dried chiles
1⅔ cups day-old breadcrumbs
4 egg whites

Heat the oil in a skillet. Add the onions, garlic, and zucchini to the skillet and cook over low heat, stirring occasionally, for 10–15 minutes, until softened and just beginning to color. Increase the heat to medium and cook for 5 minutes more, until all the moisture has been dissipated. Remove the skillet from the heat and let cool.

Meanwhile, put the carrots in a pan, add water to cover, and bring to a boil. Reduce the heat and simmer for 7 minutes, then drain, and refresh under cold water. Pat dry with paper towels.

Bring a pan of water to a boil, add the bok choy, and blanch for 1 minute. Drain well and chop.

Spoon half the zucchini mixture into a food processor. Add the bok choy, soy sauce, and chiles, process to a puree, then add the breadcrumbs and process briefly again. Scrape the mixture into a bowl and stir in the remaining zucchini mixture. Lightly beat the egg whites with a fork in a bowl and stir into the zucchini mixture.

Bring a pan of water to a boil. Line a terrine or loaf pan with wax paper; brush lightly with oil.

Spoon one-third of the zucchini mixture into the prepared terrine and spread it out evenly. Top with half the carrots. Add half the remaining zucchini mixture and spread out, then top with remaining carrots. Finally, spread the remaining zucchini mixture over them.

Brush a piece of wax paper with oil and place it on top of the mixture. Cover the terrine with a sheet of foil, tying it in place with kitchen string. Put it into a steamer and cover with a tight-fitting lid. Set the steamer over the pan and steam for 1½ hours.

Remove the terrine and let cool. Remove and discard the foil and wax paper. Cover the terrine with a lid or with plastic wrap and chill in the refrigerator for 8 hours or overnight. To serve, turn out onto a serving plate, remove and discard the lining paper, and cut into slices.

spinach & gorgonzola ravioli

SERVES 4

pasta dough
1 3/4 cups white bread flour,
   plus extra for dusting
1/2 tsp salt
2 eggs
1 tbsp olive oil

filling
8 oz/225 g spinach, trimmed
2 tbsp butter
2 shallots, finely chopped
2 oz/55 g Gorgonzola cheese,
   crumbled

1/3 cup grated Pecorino Romano
   cheese, plus extra to serve
pinch of grated nutmeg
salt and pepper
chopped parsley, to garnish

To make the pasta dough, sift the flour and salt into a bowl and make a well in the center. Add the eggs, olive oil, and 2 tablespoons of water to the well and, using your hands, gradually incorporate the dry ingredients to make an elastic dough, adding 1 tablespoon of water if necessary. Turn the dough out onto a lightly floured surface and knead well until smooth. Put into a plastic bag and let rest in the refrigerator for 45 minutes.

Cook the spinach in a little water for 4 minutes, or until just wilted. Drain and chop. Melt the butter in a pan. Cook the shallots for 5 minutes, stirring frequently. Add the spinach, cheeses, and nutmeg. Season and let cool.

Halve the pasta dough. Roll out one half on a lightly floured surface to about 1/8 inch/3 mm thick. Brush it lightly with water, then place heaped teaspoonfuls of the filling at regular intervals over it. Roll out the other piece of dough and put it on top. With floured fingers, gently press the top sheet down around the mounds of filling to seal. Cut out the ravioli with a fluted pasta cutter or a fluted cookie cutter.

Bring a large saucepan of salted water to a boil. Add the ravioli, bring back to a boil, and cook for 5 minutes. Drain well and refresh under cold water. Put into a heatproof dish or bowl that will fit inside the steamer.

Cover the steamer with a tight-fitting lid, set it over the pan of boiling water, and steam for 15 minutes. Transfer the ravioli to a warmed serving plate, garnish with chopped parsley, and serve immediately.

garbanzo beans & vegetables

SERVES 4

1 cup dried garbanzo beans,
  soaked overnight in cold water
  to cover and drained
2 tbsp olive oil
1 onion, chopped
1 garlic clove, chopped
2 celery stalks, chopped
2 carrots, chopped

1 green bell pepper, seeded and
  chopped
1 red bell pepper, seeded and
  chopped
1 small celery root, chopped
1 lb 2 oz/500 g tomatoes, peeled
  and chopped or 14 oz/400 g
  canned chopped tomatoes

$^2/_3$ cup bulgur wheat
pinch of grated nutmeg
pinch of ground cloves
$^1/_2$ tsp ground ginger
salt and pepper

Put the garbanzo beans in a large pan, add cold water to cover, and bring to a boil, then lower the heat, and simmer for $1^1/_2$ hours.

Meanwhile, heat the olive oil in a large skillet. Add the onion and garlic and cook over low heat, stirring occasionally, for 5 minutes, until softened. Add the celery, carrots, green and red bell peppers, and celery root and cook, stirring occasionally, for 5 minutes more. Stir in the tomatoes, bulgur wheat, nutmeg, cloves, and ginger and bring to a boil. Remove the skillet from the heat.

Season the vegetables with salt and pepper and spoon them into a 5-cup heatproof bowl. Put the bowl into a steamer and cover with a tight-fitting lid. Set the steamer over the pan of garbanzos and steam for 45 minutes, adding more boiling water to the garbanzos, as necessary.

Remove the steamer and drain the garbanzo beans. Stir them into the vegetables and taste and adjust the seasoning. Transfer to a warmed serving dish and serve immediately.

side dishes

chili potatoes

SERVES 4

1 lb 2 oz/500 g new potatoes
3 dried red chiles
1 tbsp hot paprika
1 tsp ground cumin
2 garlic cloves, chopped

1/2 tsp salt
2 tbsp sherry vinegar
2/3 cup olive oil

Bring a pan of water to a boil. Put the unpeeled potatoes into a steamer, cover with a tight-fitting lid, and set the steamer over the pan. Steam for about 20 minutes, until tender.

Meanwhile, make the chili sauce. Pound the chiles, paprika, and cumin seeds to a paste in a mortar with a pestle. Add the garlic and salt and continue to pound until fully incorporated. Gradually stir in the vinegar, then whisk in the oil, a little at a time.

When the potatoes are tender, remove them from the steamer and peel if you like. Put them into a warmed serving dish, pour the sauce over them, and serve immediately.

pilau rice

SERVES 4

heaping 1 cup basmati rice, rinsed
and soaked
2 tbsp sunflower oil
2 garlic cloves, finely chopped
1 onion, finely chopped
1 fresh red chile, seeded and
finely chopped

1 red bell pepper, seeded and
finely chopped
1 tsp ground cumin
$\frac{1}{2}$ tsp ground turmeric
1 tsp fennel seeds
$\frac{1}{2}$ tsp ground coriander
2 green cardamom pods, lightly
crushed

2 cloves
about 2 cups vegetable or chicken
stock or water
salt and pepper
fresh cilantro sprigs, to garnish

Drain the rice well and set aside. Heat the oil in a pan. Add the garlic, onion, chile, and bell pepper and cook over low heat, stirring occasionally, for 5 minutes, until softened. Stir in the cumin, turmeric, fennel seeds, coriander, cardamom, and cloves and cook, stirring constantly, for 1 minute, until the spices give off their aroma.

Add the rice and cook, stirring constantly, for 2–3 minutes, until opaque. Pour in enough stock or water to cover the rice by 1 inch/2.5 cm and season with salt and pepper. Bring to a boil, then reduce the heat to very low, cover with a tight-fitting lid, and steam for 20 minutes, until all the liquid has been absorbed. Do not remove the lid during cooking.

Remove the pan from the heat and let stand, without removing the lid, for 2 minutes. Uncover and fluff up the grains with a fork. Transfer to a warmed serving dish and remove and discard the cloves. Garnish with cilantro sprigs and serve immediately.

spiced saffron rice

SERVES 6

about 2 cups vegetable stock or
  water
1/2 tsp saffron threads, lightly
  crushed
1 tbsp sunflower oil

generous 1 cup basmati rice,
  rinsed and soaked
1/2 tsp salt
4 green cardamom pods

Put 3 tbsp of the stock or water into a small pan, add the saffron, and heat gently to simmering point. Remove the pan from the heat and set aside.

Drain the rice. Heat the oil in a large pan. Add the rice and cook, stirring constantly, for 2–3 minutes, until opaque. Pour in just enough stock or water to cover it by 1 inch/2.5 cm and add the salt and cardamom pods. Bring to a boil, then reduce the heat to very low, cover with a tight-fitting lid, and steam for 15 minutes. Do not remove the lid during steaming.

Add the saffron and its soaking liquid to the pan, re-cover the pan, and steam for 5–7 minutes more, until all the liquid has been absorbed.

Remove the pan from the heat and let stand, without removing the lid, for 2 minutes. Uncover the rice and fluff up the grains with a fork. Remove and discard the cardamom pods and serve immediately.

bulgur wheat with herbs

SERVES 4

2 tbsp butter
1/2 red onion, finely chopped
1 garlic clove, finely chopped
1 cup bulgur wheat
1 bay leaf
2 cups vegetable or chicken stock

4 tbsp chopped fresh parsley
4 tbsp chopped fresh mint
3 scallions, finely chopped
1/2 cup black olives
6 oz/175 g cherry tomatoes,
  halved

1/2 cup extra virgin olive oil
4 tbsp lemon juice
salt and pepper
fresh mint sprigs, to garnish

Melt the butter in a pan. Add the onion and garlic and cook over low heat, stirring occasionally, for 5 minutes, until softened. Add the bulgur wheat and bay leaf, pour in the stock, and bring to a boil. Reduce the heat to low, cover with a tight-fitting lid, and steam for 15 minutes, until all the liquid has been absorbed.

Remove the pan from the heat and spoon the bulgur wheat mixture into a bowl. Remove and discard the bay leaf. Let cool slightly, then add the parsley, mint, scallions, black olives, and tomatoes. Mix well.

Whisk together the olive oil and lemon juice in a pitcher and season with salt and pepper. Pour the dressing into the bowl and toss to mix. Serve at room temperature, garnished with mint sprigs.

couscous with nuts & dried fruit

SERVES 6

1½ cups couscous
heaping ¼ cup plumped
   dried apricots
⅓ cup blanched
   almonds

2½ cups vegetable or chicken
   stock or water
1 tsp extra virgin olive oil
2 tbsp chopped fresh cilantro
salt and pepper

Put the coucous into a bowl and pour in the amount of water recommended on the package. Let soak, stirring frequently with a fork to separate the grains, for 30 minutes, until almost all the liquid has been absorbed.

Meanwhile, using a sharp knife, cut the apricots into thin strips and set aside. Heat a heavy skillet, add the almonds, and cook over low heat, shaking the skillet frequently, for 1–2 minutes, until lightly toasted. Remove the skillet from the heat.

Pour the stock or water into a pan and bring to a boil. Line a steamer with cheesecloth. Stir the apricots into the soaked couscous, season with salt and pepper, and spoon into the steamer. Cover with a tight-fitting lid, set the steamer over the pan, and steam for 20 minutes.

Transfer the couscous mixture to a warmed serving dish and stir in the olive oil, cilantro, and almonds. Serve immediately.

peas with lettuce, shallots & mint

SERVES 6

4½ cups podded fresh peas
2 shallots, thinly sliced
1 garlic clove, finely chopped
8 romaine lettuce leaves,
    shredded

3 fresh mint sprigs, plus extra
    to garnish
1 tsp superfine sugar
2 tbsp butter or sunflower oil
salt and pepper

Bring a pan of water to a boil. Line a steamer with dampened wax paper.

Put the peas into the steamer and add the shallots, garlic, lettuce, and mint sprigs. Sprinkle with the sugar and dot with the butter or drizzle with the oil. Season with salt and pepper.

Cover the steamer with a tight-fitting lid and set the steamer over the pan. Steam for about 4–5 minutes, until the peas are tender.

Remove and discard the mint sprigs. Transfer the vegetables to a warm serving dish and serve immediately with fresh mint to garnish.

glazed carrots & parsnips

SERVES 4–6

2$\frac{1}{2}$ cups vegetable stock or
    water
3 tbsp honey
4 tbsp toasted sesame seeds

16 baby carrots, trimmed
8 baby parsnips, trimmed and
    cut lengthwise
salt and pepper

Pour the stock or water into a large pan and bring to a boil. Meanwhile, pour the honey into a small pan and heat gently until just warm. Alternatively, heat briefly in a bowl in the microwave. Remove from the heat.

Spread out the sesame seeds on a shallow plate. Brush the carrots and parsnips all over with the honey, then roll them in the sesame seeds.

Put the vegetables in a steamer in a single layer and cover with a tight-fitting lid. Set the steamer over the pan and steam for 20–25 minutes, until the vegetables are tender. Serve immediately.

desserts

rich crème brûlée with exotic fruit

SERVES 6

2 cups heavy cream
4 egg yolks
2 tbsp superfine sugar
¼ tsp vanilla extract
1 banana

lemon juice, for brushing
1 small mango, peeled, pitted, and
   chopped
2 kiwis, peeled and chopped
2 tbsp chopped preserved ginger

¼ cup raw brown sugar
¼ cup walnut halves, finely
   chopped

Pour the cream into a small pan and bring to just below boiling point. Meanwhile, beat together the egg yolks and superfine sugar until pale and creamy. Gradually stir in the cream until thoroughly combined, then stir in the vanilla extract.

Bring a pan of water to a boil. Meanwhile, peel the banana, brush with lemon juice, and slice into a bowl. Add the mango, kiwis, and ginger and mix well.

Divide the fruit equally among 6 ramekins, then pour the egg custard over it. Cover the ramekins with plastic wrap, put in a steamer, and cover with a tight-fitting lid. Place the steamer over the pan and steam for 10–15 minutes, until set.

Remove the ramekins from the steamer and remove and discard the plastic wrap, then let cool. Cover with fresh plastic wrap and chill in the refrigerator for at least 4 hours.

Preheat the broiler. Combine the raw brown sugar and chopped nuts in a small bowl. Remove and discard the plastic wrap and sprinkle the nut mixture over the top of the desserts. Place the ramekins under the broiler for 2–3 minutes, until the tops are caramelized and golden, turning occasionally so that they brown evenly. Chill in the refrigerator for at least 2 hours, until the caramel is crisp.

light-as-air fruit sponge cake with hot fruit coulis

SERVES 4

5 mandarin oranges
sunflower oil, for brushing
2 tsp dark corn syrup
1 banana
1 tsp lemon juice
heaping 1 cup self-raising flour

$^1/_4$ cup finely ground Brazil nuts
$1^1/_2$ cups fresh white
   breadcrumbs
scant $^1/_2$ cup superfine sugar
7 tbsp milk

hot fruit coulis
2 passion fruit
1 mango, peeled, pitted,
   and chopped
6 tbsp mandarin juice

Finely grate the rind of 2 mandarins and squeeze out the juice. Peel the remaining mandarins, removing all traces of pith. Cut them into thin slices with a sharp knife.

Brush a $1^3/_4$-pint/1-liter ovenproof bowl with oil and spoon in the corn syrup. Arrange the mandarin slices in the bowl and set aside. Bring a saucepan of water to a boil.

Peel the banana and mash with the lemon juice. Sift the flour into a bowl and stir in the nuts, breadcrumbs, sugar, and grated rind. Stir in the milk and enough juice to make a firm mixture. Spoon into the bowl and level the top.

Cut out circles of wax paper and foil, 2 inches/5 cm larger than the top of the bowl, put them together, and make a pleat in the center. Cover the bowl, foil side uppermost, and tie in place. Put the bowl in a steamer and cover with a tight-fitting lid. Set over the pan of boiling water and steam for $1^3/_4$ hours.

Meanwhile, make the coulis. Halve the passion fruit and scoop out the pulp and seeds into a blender or food processor. Add the mango, mandarin juice, and 3 tablespoons of water. Process until smooth. Pass the coulis through a nylon strainer into a bowl and set aside.

Just before serving, gently heat the coulis in a small saucepan. Remove the sponge cake from the steamer, discard the covering, and turn out. Serve, handing around the hot coulis separately.

hazelnut cloud

SERVES 4

unsalted butter, for greasing
4 eggs, separated
2/3 cup superfine sugar
1 1/4 cups heavy cream

1 cup ground hazelnuts
finely grated rind of 1 lemon
pinch of ground allspice

Generously grease a 6-inch/15-cm soufflé dish with butter. Cut a double strip of wax paper long enough to go around the circumference of the dish with a 2-inch/5-cm overlap and deep enough to stand 2 inches/5 cm above the rim. Tie the strip around the outside of the dish with kitchen string.

Using an electric mixer, beat together the egg yolks and superfine sugar until pale and creamy and the whisk leaves a ribbon trail when it is lifted. Pour in the cream and whisk until thickened. Fold in the hazelnuts, lemon rind, and allspice.

Stiffly whisk the egg whites in a grease-free bowl, then gently fold into the egg yolk mixture with a flexible spatula. Gently scrape the mixture into the prepared soufflé dish.

Put the dish into a large pan and pour in enough boiling water to come about halfway up the side. Cover with a tight-fitting lid and steam very gently for 45 minutes.

Lift the dish out of the pan. Remove and discard the paper collar and serve immediately.

pears in red wine sauce

SERVES 4

grated rind and juice of 1 orange
1 1/4 cups red wine
3 tbsp honey
1 cinnamon stick
1 vanilla bean

1/2 tsp apple pie spice
1 clove
4 firm, ripe pears
1/2 tsp arrowroot or potato flour
whipped cream, to serve (optional)

Bring a pan of water to a boil. Meanwhile, put the orange rind and juice, wine, honey, cinnamon stick, vanilla bean, apple pie spice, and clove in a pan and bring to a boil, stirring frequently, then remove the pan from the heat.

Peel the pears, leaving the stem intact, and cut off a small slice from the bottom so that they will stand upright. Put them into a heatproof bowl and pour the wine mixture over them. Cover the bowl with a sheet of foil and tie in place with kitchen string.

Put the bowl into the steamer and cover with a tight-fitting lid. Set the steamer over the pan and steam for 35–40 minutes, until the pears are tender.

Remove the bowl from the steamer and let cool completely. Transfer the pears to a serving dish, standing them upright. Remove and discard the cinnamon stick, vanilla bean, and clove from the wine mixture and pour it into a small pan. Bring to a boil and cook until reduced to about 2/3 cup. Reduce the heat to a simmer.

Put the arrowroot or potato flour into a small bowl and stir in 2 tbsp of the wine sauce to make a paste. Stir the paste into the pan and simmer gently, stirring constantly, for 2 minutes, until the sauce has thickened. Remove the pan from the heat and let cool.

Pour the wine sauce over the pears and chill in the refrigerator for at least 3 hours before serving with whipped cream, if you like.

traditional toffee pudding

SERVES 4–6

1/2 cup walnut halves	3/4 cup unsalted butter	2 eggs, lightly beaten
sunflower oil, for brushing	4 tbsp heavy cream	1 cup self-rising flour
3/4 cup dark brown sugar	2 tbsp lemon juice	

Heat a heavy skillet, add the walnuts, and cook, shaking the skillet frequently, for a few minutes, until lightly toasted. Remove the skillet from the heat and let cool, then chop the nuts.

Brush a 3 3/4-cup heatproof bowl with oil. Sprinkle half the chopped walnuts over the bottom.

Put 1/4 cup the sugar, 1/4 cup of the butter, the cream, and half the lemon juice into a small pan and heat gently, stirring constantly, until the butter has melted, the sugar has dissolved, and the mixture is smooth. Remove the pan from the heat and pour half the sauce into the bowl, then swirl gently to coat the side. Reserve the remaining sauce in the pan.

Put the remaining sugar and butter into a bowl and beat until pale and fluffy. Gradually beat in the eggs, a little at a time. Sift the flour over the mixture and fold in with a flexible spatula, then fold in the remaining walnuts and the remaining lemon juice.

Bring a pan of water to a boil. Meanwhile, spoon the mixture into the bowl. Cut out a circle of wax paper 2 inches/5 cm larger than the circumference of the top of the bowl. Make a pleat in the middle, cover the bowl, and tie in place with kitchen string.

Put the bowl into a steamer and cover with a tight-fitting lid. Steam for 1 1/2 hours. Just before you are ready to serve, reheat the remaining sauce until warm.

Remove and discard the wax paper. Run a round-bladed knife around the inside of the bowl, place a warmed serving plate on top, and, holding them together, invert. Pour the remaining sauce over the dessert and serve immediately.

gooey chocolate & almond dessert

SERVES 6

heaping 1/2 cup unsalted butter,
  plus extra for greasing
2/3 cup superfine sugar
6 day-old ladyfingers
3 oz/85 g semisweet chocolate,
  broken into pieces

6 eggs, separated
3/4 cup ground almonds
cream, to serve (optional)

chocolate & brandy sauce
4 tbsp unsalted butter

heaping 1/2 cup superfine sugar
4 oz/115 g semisweet chocolate,
  broken into pieces
1/4 cup milk
2 tbsp brandy

Bring a saucepan of water to a boil. Grease a 1-quart/1.2-liter ovenproof bowl with butter and sprinkle with 1 tablespoon of the sugar. Break up the ladyfingers and crush.

Melt the chocolate in a heatproof bowl set over a saucepan of barely simmering water, stirring occasionally. Set aside to cool slightly.

Beat the remaining butter and the remaining sugar in a bowl until light and fluffy. Gradually beat in the egg yolks, then the chocolate. Fold in the crumbs and almonds. Stiffly whisk the egg whites and fold them into the mixture. Spoon into the bowl and smooth the surface.

Cut out circles of wax paper and foil 2 inches/ 5 cm larger than the circumference of the top of the bowl and put them together. Grease the paper and make a pleat in the center of both circles. Cover the bowl, foil side up, and tie in place with kitchen string. Put it into a steamer, cover with a lid, and set over the pan of boiling water. Steam for 1 hour.

To make the sauce, melt the butter and sugar in a small saucepan, stirring constantly. Remove from the heat. Melt the chocolate in a heatproof bowl set over a saucepan of simmering water. Stir in the butter mixture, then gradually stir in the milk, 1/4 cup of water, and the brandy. Remove from the heat.

Lift the bowl out of the steamer and discard the covers. Turn out the dessert, pour over the sauce, and serve with cream, if using.

chocolate & cherry delights

SERVES 4

heaping ¹⁄₂ cup unsalted butter, softened, plus extra for greasing
¹⁄₂ cup dark brown sugar
1 ripe pear

heaping ¹⁄₂ cup black cherries, pitted and halved
³⁄₄ cup all-purpose flour
3 tbsp unsweetened cocoa
¹⁄₂ tsp baking powder

2 eggs, lightly beaten
1 tsp Kirsch
2 tbsp honey
4 oz/115 g semisweet chocolate

Bring a pan of water to a boil. Generously grease 4 individual heatproof bowls, about 1 cup each, with butter. Sprinkle a little sugar in each to coat all over the insides and tip out any excess.

Peel, core, and dice the pear and put it into a bowl. Add the cherries and mix well. Divide the fruit equally among the prepared bowls.

Sift together the flour, unsweetened cocoa, and baking powder into a large bowl and add the remaining sugar, ¹⁄₂ cup of the butter, and the eggs. Beat well with an electric mixer until thoroughly combined and smooth.

Spoon the mixture into the bowls, dividing it equally among them. Cut out 4 wax and 4 foil circles 1¹⁄₂ inches/4 cm larger than the circumference of the tops of the bowls. Holding the circles together, make a pleat in the middle and cover the bowls, foil circle up, and tie in place with kitchen string.

Put the bowls in a steamer and cover with a tight-fitting lid. Set the steamer over the pan and steam for 45 minutes.

Just before the end of the cooking time, put the remaining butter in a small pan with the Kirsch and honey. Break the chocolate into pieces and add to the pan, then heat gently, stirring constantly, until melted and smooth.

Lift the bowls out of the steamer and remove and discard the wax and foil circles. Run a round-bladed knife around the bowls to loosen. One at a time, place an individual serving plate over a bowl and, holding the two together, invert. Pour the chocolate and honey sauce over the desserts and serve immediately.